# CAPTIVE

# CAPTIVE

## AMY HOLMAN

SADDLE ROAD PRESS

Captive © Amy Holman 2023

Saddle Road Press
Ithaca, New York
saddleroadpress.com

Book design by Don Mitchell
Cover artwork by Amy Holman

ISBN 9798987954102
Library of Congress Control Number: 2023939713

Books by Amy Holman
*Wrens Fly Through This Opened Window*
*Wait for Me, I'm Gone*
*The Cathedral of My Head*
*tissue and bone*
*Dwelling with Fire*

# Contents

## SNOWIES AND BLUES

Where there is no accumulation, laced and soft, come flocks
of snowies to shrub pine, wetlands and dock.

Is it a wish to speak a season's complete possibility, or make
familiar an inclination to leave? Snowy egrets could be milk or paint
egrets, trillium or salt egrets. But they descend softly,

long necks and wing fans. Each one a blizzard
in a nickname. Is it their lurking extinction, their long,

millennial disintegration that turns blue whales to blues
on our tongues? When they call it tracking blues — passing
sonar over the hemispheres one by one and ticking off
fewer mammals than a population can trust, do they know

they're speaking double? Whose blues permeate this air,
whose mammal memory haunts farthest?

## SOCIAL STUDIES

Imagine watching from history and geometry
the performance art of preteen Christos
wrapping stakes with crepe paper
into life-size whales aswim on the dips and swells
of well-kept lawns. I was out with flu and missed
that day in 6th grade when trios of the other girls
mapped school grounds with oceans of rights,
humpbacks, blue, and, giggling, sperm.
I'd switched from public the spring before,
and still hovered between its teases and new stares.
Teacher told two mean girl friends to guide my charting
near the tulip tree. I was scared but they were sullen.
I had the tools, and measurements of the whale,
I had the grass and soft earth, curiosity.

I had the grass and soft earth, curiosity,
the sun had dried days of rain. Besides showing us,
through petitions and campaigns to save an animal, how
grassroots movements work, our teacher assigned
the shy girl a giant to make, and the girls
whose years-long union stood frail, the task
of working together to see a bigger picture.
My whale was the length of middle school.
Just one. How big the ocean, the earth. The girls
who used to stare and snicker were too hurt to think
of me. Whatever it was breaking the bond between them
would. When they said *step inside,* I left them
for the confines of my blue whale. Just one, just me.
Imagine watching, from history, this geometry.

## Retreat

Biking along Dune Drive's dark greens—bayberry, a few spruce—
you could not see our house tucked there. One red rugosa flirted
at the fence even we could not see from the house.

Pedaling home, once, against traffic, my brother and I spotted toadlets
in a hopping bloom—wayward, flinging bodies advancing into cars—
and we stopped our bikes. Hard to see their dark jacquard

on the asphalt, but we hemmed their bolt. This was long before the brazen
blaze that zapped our house into vapor, and hippocamps. This was when
toads, in a chorus line, sang to us at night from the window box.

The babies were the size of toads for Barbies, very small, precisely formed.
The cars must sound like ocean, garrulous with the shore. Shifting
our wheels, we halted toad dispersal, and our matched panic,

precisely formed for later reference. What more might be unknown, not saved?
Guides to a generation between traffic and the Atlantic, we reoriented them
to their scrubby, hot dunes, wild carrot, and sea percussion, and

returned to play on dunes, ride breaking waves, and drop off to bedtime
toads the size of Hot Wheels, bayberry and sea sprucing the air.
The ocean drove all night. Just a couple of Junes with Toad

Broadway before the black rat snakes arrived, and the lights went out.
Long before a blaze untucked that house with 40-foot flames above
the dunes, as seen by a lone bicyclist pedaling by that cold night.

## No One There

This was before the house we had went up in flames
on that refuge in the dunes on the barrier isle
and when I could not be more than wind

rattling the screened door to my friends' house.
I played each day with the youngest two across from us,
which was long before the house we had went up in flames

in an unsolved crime of real estate envy, struck mid-
winter when no one was there. Why so shy? I can't say.
That I could not be more than wind

still rattles me. A voice—their older sibling, too lazy
to descend—calls down, Who's there? I can't say, too shy.
This was before the house we had went up in flames

in an unkempt and belittling blaze brazen between
the wetlands and the vast Atlantic with its softening air.
And how could I be not more than wind

knocking, I ask my child self who persevered
and still got trapped waiting until I was seen.
This was before it all went up in flames
and when I could not be more than wind.

## I'M A RABBIT GIRL,

she says, and it's a child you see
in a room full of bunny toys and art,

not a music teacher in her mid-thirties
in Brooklyn, defending herself to the press
after the arrest. They need to be wild,

she says, of the meat rabbits saved
from butchers, the lab testers, Netherland

dwarfs and Belgian hares who listened
to her flute, but you'd see a tasty meadow
with burrows and buttercups, maybe

her grandmother's farm in Poland, not
182 cold bunnies huddled behind chipped

wood in an unused tire yard. They need to be
wild game for the zoo lions, she also said once—
to her shame—perhaps when the monthly

multiplications troubled a limited space
and budget. Rabbit girl could not see her way

clear, in her failed million dollar, pastel Easter
Bunny breeding project she later passed off
as an attempt to develop a children's

bunny garden under the F/G overpass. To be
caging leporidae—as she had with a fraction—

in a padlocked shed on the Gowanus auto
strip, hops in the face of flutey rabbit girl's

pastel lion luncheon community. But then,
you can see that, with the herd biting
and raping each other and contracting syphilis,

that special, confidential quality that her first
rabbit, Snowflake, shared with Rabbit Girl,

was diminished. She's to be caged for 45 days,
kept from owning rabbits for five years, and
see a shrink about collecting. She's resisting

with a suit against the bunny activists and
the ASPCA who, anyone can see,

do not want people owning animals,
which, by the way, she didn't, because you
can't own what is wild, or what needs to be.

## THE HEART IS QUIET

Why did the dog in Trinidad return to the burning house
after he saved his sleeping man? *Nobody else inside,* the man said,
yet his dog ran back. Even a scientist reportedly mourned the death

of the parrot in her lab when she knew he was not a colleague
with whom to lunch. Dogs make distinctions, too. We're not them,
obviously, but they try not to make us feel on the fringe

because of it, even if we can fly off the handle. In the ashes
were the bodies of the dog and parrot. (The man in his kitchen,
his bird remarking, the dog dancing toward a morsel, guests

arriving. Such bustle and color in the heart, everyone talking
and eating.) *Is there anyone else inside,* they asked the choking man
when his dog ran back. He made the wrong distinction.

# BIRD HEARTS RACING

Already, chestnut-bellied finches know confinement—
held in men's hands—plus, confusing wind, without their wing dips

buffeted, when 34 are slotted in orange hair rollers, packed
in a duffle carry-on, and flown to New York for bird racing.

Not a contest of flight speeds, for wouldn't they always be taking it
too far, undulating over each finish line and into canopies

of the Parks Department's plantings? It's a competition of paired
male songbirds—finches superior to any other—singing to

win men thousands or hundreds, owners or bettors. Bird emotions
are controversial to some humans who specify these residual

dinosaurs, yet the four-chambered hearts do allow fear.
In Guyana, a man bicycles through heavily degraded former forest

with a finch in his fist. The engine of the heart ignites in the breeze
and wings agitate a palm. Man in a room plays a tape of the teeeyeees

and teeeyooos of the last winning finch, training his capture
to sing the same best. Finches will want someone, they will tire

of cover tunes. Where are their burds, these birds must wonder,
their perfected songs of prowess and pure love exploding

in the quiet air? In the remaining forests, the shes tune their ears
to untutored males, each pair enraptured by their specificity.

# CONTRIBUTOR

I step into the problems of the particles,
as coffee powder puffs onto my contact lenses.

Eyelids flutter, rinsing grit with tears that,
under microscope, look unlike basal weeps
of maintenance; they are my reflex cries.

Each drop's image will differ, as do frosted leaves,
and urban ports, that tear photographer proved.

The unseen's art and design department, chooses
strengths of salt, lipids, potassium, immunoglobulins,
for instant display ads for joy, upset, hilarity, moisture.

Beautiful and bright, small and great, there's no
vista too miniature for our inquiry. I resume

my quest for coffee to go without marine littering
plastic lid, yet keeping intact the paper cup's
catastrophe of forest, and caffeine's blight of night.

No plant will take root on that plastic island
three times the size of continental France.

I contribute to its future mounds with maintenance:
mini rewetting lens droppers, ballpoint pen cartridges,
toothpaste's micro plastics, plus the tubes, and

brush bristles. Innovation visits the young
who think outside the non-biodegradable box,

such as Boyan Slat, who left his pursuit of aerospace,
at 17, to clean the ocean of its buoyant, man-made trash.
He set in motion Pacific Ocean participation: currents

sweep inside a solar powered fence. All things
wise and wonderful, it works, except on micro beads.

These should be caught in screens attached
to sewers, says a turtle activist standing instead
on Oregon beaches gathering his heaped

electrostatic nets. He can't stand
there forever. Bits poison zooplankton

that now disown food, and welcome plastic,
flight response to fear consumed. Tiny parts
of the diminishing food chain, they measure death

in growing swallows. Cities will also bury
recycling. And we hold archipelagos of plastic

in our rivers, surgeons found out in half
their blood donors. Refuse the refuse never possible.
I'd like to believe in us, except that microbes

like *Ideonella sakaiensis*, entering stage left,
to eat water bottles fed it outside Japan's recycling

plant, seem much more capable. How great
is earth almighty if unmade and unwell?
I step into the part I cull from the problem.

## A Small Invasion

Atlantic has the salt to stanch a wound,
partially purifying the canal
of heavy metals, gonorrhea, muck.
In a few years, the oyster beds will be
placed, but a dying dolphin attempting
to beach will still be sorry it strayed to
Gowanus; death ought to be clean. Canal
and ocean rose past the banks of cattails,
spent condoms and raccoon dung. We watched as
it sluiced across the 3rd Street Bridge, and slid
downhill to Bond Street's new gurgling brook.
Bond aptly dead-ends the canal's west bend,
also a dead end that has risen tonight
with Sandy, high winds, sputtering rainfall.

With Sandy, high winds, sputtering rainfall,
and myriad bacterium strains, it's
astounding that the unmarked black cab drove
straight into the downslope depth of 3rd
and two guys chose to wade thigh deep into
their near future deterioration.
*Go to the hospital,* a neighbor yelled.
Most likely insurance fraud to get new
wheels, man got busted by the moon. Unlike
Red Hook and Manhattan's lower east side
turned inlets instead of streets, just past
midnight, low tide takes it all back. Not that
Bond should bond with anyone's soles, paws, but
Atlantic leaves the salt to stanch a wound.

## How to Make a Whale Out of an Envelope

Start with a #10 business size
and roll your pen from jaw to fluke.
I think a humpback is easy to draw
with the spine along the fold.
But you could choose the killer.

To say this oil spill is a killer
is apt though BP likes to downsize
catastrophe—make six or seven folds
on warnings and shove them in a pocket. A fluke
is a barb, a harpoon that will draw

blood, a different kind of spill. Draw
the dorsal fin of the killer
whale before you do the fluke.
It's a sharper angle of size
on the envelope flap you unfold.

Cut a blowhole in the fold
of a #10 on the crease. Now draw
the mouth that seems to smile. A ten size
death is decimate—gulf bleeds to sea—a killer
reduction. An oil spill is not a fluke

in a business without precautions. A fluke
slapped on the sea can be SOS. As waves fold
dispersants into gasoline, and petroleum in pelican eggs, the killer
changes form. Bluefin in cardiac arrest. Now draw
the blind eye. We were too in love with tank size

reads our epitaph. Evolution makes a killer fold—shrimp without eyes.
I can't draw a breath in the size of all our dying. Survival is a fluke.

# FIELDS OF LONELINESS

*A cereal, a legume, time to fill our jowls, night without light,*
lobbied the disruptors, unheard in the whir of farms and generation,
until activists knelt down. France landed in the European Court

of Justice for endangering that pest, the Great Hamster of Alsace.
With black fur dickey and pale, graceful hands, a rodent that hibernates
misted woods and frosty plains adrift in foaming white fog to awaken

renewed, desirous, and faint, it can't eat corn or bring forth
when highways supplant fields. Farmers scoffed, but single crop
reliance blights the ground. France had to resow cereals for the plaintiffs,

or be fined millions. Imagine Alsatian hamsters in the golden towers;
can't you hear them squeak amid the multi-lingual judgments?
*Flushing bars on mowers, please, and intercrop covers,* they requested.

Luxembourg ruled that same year against nations returning refugees
to homelands. Where we belong is who we are. Wouldn't anyone
under threat—displaced rodent and human, equal—speak loudest?

*Even poppies give awning for our yawning.* France set its biodiversity
plan for its depleted great hamsters in farmlands: strips of alfalfa grow
between the maize for picky, solo, burrowing eaters, sized—and shaped—

like large aubergines. The grass waves above their stuffing, to conceal
vulnerability. But their sums don't rise in this resolution of scarcity
and relations; fields too few, night skies refused darkness,

circadian rhythms falling prey to cacophony, esurient eagles and
famished foxes, plus female hamsters fighting males that smell wrong.
Who we are is where we'll be—extinction list, or here for now.

# Goat Gardeners Take the High Ground
# in Brooklyn Bridge Park

*—Brooklyn Heights Patch* headline, June 24, 2016

Horatio, Hector, Minnie & Eyebrows graze on language
opposing change—"economic & environmental harm to natives"
in a borough almost bursting with *arrival*—

> great word from the Old French, *ad ripam*,
> to the riverbank—

in a new public park beside a loud expressway and an eastern river.
No more broad leaf invasives out to "displace & threaten stability,"

no more Japanese honeysuckle or poison ivy, each as delicious a *repast*—

> Middle English derivative of Old French & Latin, *pastus*,
> fodder—the go-to goats prove.

Just now, the news is overgrown with the raw material of hate,
expressions of war & difference in our words, made worse
by a recent campaign allowed to flourish like a rosa multiflora on a berm.

The root of *word*—

> same as rose, Proto-Indo-European, *wrdho*, thorn, bramble,
> also same as verb, *were*, speak, to say—

is both prickly & showy, refuge & barrier.

Our culture is cross with its *roads*—before 900, Middle & Old English, *rad*,

> a riding journey on horseback—bursting with a *rival* mentality,
> except that Latin, *rivalis*,
> one who uses a stream in common
> with another, reads as accepted as a neighbor.

I like the goats' good work this summer devouring the bullies
that block the sun and strangle their neighbors when left
to grow wild—even the honeysuckle with its brief, sweet expressions.

Not that there ever was any such thing as invading in moderation,
but the zebra mussels originating in Russia that consume

the algae the fish want to eat—the fish that we want to eat—
also filter toxins from our lakes.

We want to protect the honeybees that are foreign to our continent;
we like their product and their industry, pollinating the plants
that sustain us. Do we consider indigenous bees—

we many who are not native to this continent, arriving
on whale roads to make industry a faith?

Who erects the infinite sky wall?

Not the *mustang*—
          wild, having no master—introduced tame to
                    the Great Plains by Spanish conquistadors,
and now

an exotic, non-native the U.S. Department of Fish & Wildlife want out.

Yet, equus began 4,000,000 years ago in North America
& before dying out in the late Pleistocene, made roads to Eurasia
on land bridges.

The masterless, we learn, is both

emigrant & immigrant

unlike the domestic *goat* from Southwestern Asia & Eastern Europe,
whose root name, *capra aegagrus hircus*—
     goat wild goat domestic goat—
needs grazing.

# FRET

Mid-winter, a fishing boat launches off beach in dawn's
pastel sea fret. I spot a humpback breach at 7:44, first of our day,
and deep enough out that an eight-story building could stand,
golden cow-nosed ray skimming its roof. I'm taking the notes—
water temp, Beaufort scale, geographic coordinates, glare.
Red-billed tropicbirds zoom past with long wisps of snowy plumes.
This domain is leading. Without bombarding tech and attending to-do,
my mind's not a fretwork of distraction. This is the zone I'll protect,
where pan-tropical spotted dolphins vie for fish, manta rays
in conjugal tiers fly and skiff the Pacific, Magnificent Frigatebirds
stay with infinite currents. Hey, ocean, as we drop the hydrophone
and listen for song circulated from sinus to bone to larynx
in the whale poised upside down for querulous coos
and Orbison purrs—like fingers pressing the fret—I'm all yours.

NATURE

The Internet is confused
by the news. What is a wombat

doing in a net on the right
ad column of Facebook? Abe

Vigoda has died. A wombat
was fished out of a Tasmanian lake.

Abe Vigoda joined Phish
onstage in 2013 dressed as a wombat

during the Phish song "Wombat"
about Abe Vigoda as Fish. Many

wombats at once is a mob,
and angered, any wombat will let

the enemy in, then crush its
skull. It was only business, Tessio said.

## My Mother Contributes to Force and Reaction

Not my bird's nest, she said to the young real estate agent on an errand for an unnamed buyer, sun tanning her skin as she reclined with an issue of *Vogue* or *Time* on her deck in the small town named for a Celtic paradise for the knights of the roundtable. No one else was there, and besides, it was her decision, the house in her name. Just that weekend when we were all there, flocks of tired and talkative passerines had lined the telephone wires, roof edge, deck railings and shrub pine tips to change feathers. House sparrows, marsh wrens, pine siskins? Could hardly see out to the brushstroke sea in its dark September hue, its arching olive and ruffling salt breakers.

Vulnerable, she was, but in the future tense, not with this messenger her nephew's age. Nestled in the peaceful Tuesday, with gusts scattering things months away, she'd not meant to receive anyone in her bathing suit, though it had its own skirt, a delicate wave of Lycra below her waist fluttering free of its modus to stretch. She was not like the rest of us who actually body surfed the coastal Atlantic, but she did like negative ions lifting the mood. What music was playing? Not Donna Summer's heavy breathing wafting over the dunes to the neighbors in the years that was embarrassing. Maybe Anne Murray, Willie Nelson, Django Reinhardt spinning on my old high school stereo, the future tense of which was a stylus needle in a melted plastic shell.

That refusal to let go of something someone else wanted — beachfront property, not the graying brown mid-c mod built on the sand like a plus sign — brought a gale force wind to our lives, disheveling it and leaving it that way, as we dispersed from the ash. How was it that she had no right in what was hers? The next migration, birds arrived to moult on the kinesis of invisible house.

# MY MOTHER MADE HERSELF THE DEER WITH A BROKEN LEG

We saw a deer through the pane into someone else's yard.
The leg moved like a tube sock pinned to the hip
and half filled with sticks. I did not like to see it suffer,

either. She was upset — my mother — that no one helped
the doe. Was it a mother, too? As if we were the first
to observe the scene. We weren't. All had been told

to let her be. My mother had suffered a destruction
of the self, a divorce, and *no one cared*. That wasn't true.
We were grown, on our own. I agree it was hard. Yet

in those moments of a cold November day, we watched
a doe, disabled and enduring, walk across a yard and eat
a hedge. I wish she could have seen it like that.

## The Hollow

Even with the blade of Amtrak speeding the middle rail,
that incandescent and empty south-going MetroNorth platform
in any weather seemed as removed from consciousness
as a photograph stuck in a drawer.

A Canada goose welcomed me each Monday night with trochees
of territorial honks near the moored sailboats, after my footfalls across
the transom and down stairs ended near the tip of the platform.

By the time the golden links of my 9:04 train rounded a distant
bend of the Hudson route, I belonged to the confidence
of tide-lapping boats and snoozing goose.
The hollow is a cup of sleep.

Then a car drove onto the night-swallowed slip of road
between platform and river at a strolling pace, and its driver stopped
to idle near the short set of stairs to me. A pale man in a beige Ford.

It loosened from my ribcage a fluttering ache of capture
adjacent to the minutes away ride to Grand Central.
My Canadian slept on the river with one eye
open to his own predators.

The driver reversed. Did he note my disquiet, or hear the harmonic horn
of the local closing an opportunity. The mind soothes and ruins.
The hollow was cup, the hollow is rift.

The photograph was torn with the opening of the drawer.

VESTIGE

I think about how the Scottish artist Rob
Mulholland installs mirrored men and women

in fields and forest that blend in like windows
into it until, it figures, what it is really about

is looking back, and too, how, that afternoon
ten years and two seasons on, the arson

investigator at the steering wheel told me
that firemen I said sat vigil on the smoldering

house to stop sparks devouring the isle through
a taste for dune grass, likely hold evidence —

trace chemical and psychological ash—
to construe who, what and why, no matter

that they never came forward with these vestiges
of inhabiting through erasure. Cool collectors

of smudge and flicker, remnant minerals,
organic residue, charcoal. Let me sketch

with that burnt vine, those blackened stairs,
the ones we didn't see near us, outlines glinting.

## Reckless Endangerment

*"All I wanted was a Garden of Eden." —Antoine Yates*

A photographer must be on the escape—
to capture this shot of an NYPD officer
propped mid-air in blue headgear, sleeves rolled
to bare arms bearing arms. Offbeat, this beat.
There's no surprising Ming, who stands
with his white belly bulged against smogged glass—
a man with arms raised to unfasten sash,
but for his giant, whiskered head, agape with fangs.
The cop's nape is flushed. He's close enough
to shake the big cat's paw. Sleep hunts
neurotransmitters in Ming's blood and brain
since the cop's concoction pierced his fur.
I hear that wheezing rage purr scattering
through architecture's bind, and human rules.

What a bind are these human rulers, architects
of docility and danger. A tiger chomped
his man's thigh, and paused. Despite blood
tasting on his tongue, he listened to commands
he'd heard all year, and un-bit mid-maul.
Even tigers wrestle with consciousness.
Ming lunged at the kitten, not really
for the man who mothered him in a room.
But Antoine fled his Eden, claimed,
to suspicious ER physicians measuring bites
and calling authorities, a pit bull attacked.
Mudflats on river and snowy tundra runs,
blood whispered to its captive cayman alligator
and Siberian-Bengal big cat to live inside
their minds, their instincts, and not as captives.

Minds are captive agitators, instinct
another trap when wild animals
have their own four walls with carpet, wrong
climates and views to Harlem's endless brick.
But tropical and Midwest sanctuaries loomed.
Not tundra, but grassy Ohio with former circus cats.
Antoine was held at Rikers, but sued the city
for the disappearance of his rabbit—
Judge said, *take that up with the alligator.*
He took the freight of recklessly
endangering shared by his mother,
who looked after kids—the human kind,
not goat—while a growing tiger strolled
the halls of predatorial ennui.

And we are predatorial,
deadly. I kept expecting another outcome
after the image of a police officer
rappelling a building in the projects
with a rifle-shaped tranquilizer gun,
emerged in the paper. How long before it
imprinted on our conscious, culture?
Still, Caroline Domingo once came home to 5E
after long hours sewing, to see Ming loose
and lumbering past the room she had rented
from Antoine. *I'm not seeing this*, she thought,
weary, terrified. Yet she went on in,
soon accepting the wild for who it was—
it was all of them, and kin.

Who is it? All of us, we are kin, said
Mitochondrial Eve, having felt at once herself,
and not, her new energy metabolism starting
to crochet a chain of mothers 200,000 years long.
Sun bright or scarce, plates cracked and drifted,
we are linked in pigmented and depigmented
genes across migration's map, if you recall.
All we know is who we are and how we are treated.
We know the tigers live in American zoos
and black market trades, Asian swamps and
rainforest. We know the Siberian is 95.6 percent
encased in kitty. Rappel means "to recall" and
spiraling ropes bring us into view, outsiders
to ourselves. The demographer is about to escape.

## Let Them Be Endangered

There's a conflagration in phrasing—the terms that kill or save—
and biologists sit vigil on the ruin: *functionally extinct*,
says the koala advocate down under. Viral and infectious, words change us.
Biologists say not to give up, that *functionally* displaces promise.
    Let them be *endangered*.

Be vigilant against our ruin. Note the cycle of death within life;
retroviral infections changed us. A placenta functioned
as promise—begun in koalas from the shell of a retrovirus in primeval days,
    it replicated in us.

We'd like to make language deny that koalas succumb to damage
and blaze. Yet, southern koalas blaze through damages.
A generational death kills some, mutates in others: their cancer DNAs
    get snipped at the waist.

We'll cancel their deaths—snip snip, no waste—except
for elements combusting down south. Remember
when they used to be bears? Not. Remember to bear the loss responsibly.
It's not easy to admit our contributions to destruction
    in this conflagration of phrasing.

PLENTY

Already it's weird that we can reach out and touch them,
grey whales swimming close enough to our little boats
to be stroked, frequently, often, every day of their annual

affection phase, winter in Baja California, when we're told
that one likes to lift small craft to take for rides on her broad
belly. And, here she is, Valentina—named once by a man,

of course—aligning her aural midriff in the green lagoon
under the five of us, and flexing her wing-fins. She leverages
and lolls. We choral. Her 70,000 pounds could chuck us

skyward if she wanted. We're fine, forgiven. At the bow,
I look for where to grip, but our teaser just bumps us
with her womb—a body wink—and we are slow wobble.

I'm relief and disappointment twinned. In the body of water
where her ancestors were bled by our barbs to the disruption
of their species, she rolls and rises lee side, rests her underbite

the size of a seed furrow just like my tabby indicating where
she wants the rub. Skin to skin, we get each other. She's sleek
as an inner tube. These are protected waters where humans

can't interfere. Every grey tries again to be alive, mating
and bearing young in the warm bowl of currents fed by Pacific
sluicing over sandbars. These are barriers the greys know

are inscrutable to wounding, echolocating, calf-hungry
orcas, those big pie-bald dolphins who may yet get
the chance to kill at the grey whale vulnerability juncture

off Monterey Bay, if ships don't strike, and nets don't strangle.
Valentina is pregnant, we understand, and going for plenty.
It's one way resistance behaves.

## DRAWING OUT A DRAWSKA VAMPIRE

A sickle collar for the cholera sickened,
he held a mouthful of fear. Rocked by reproach
for expiring quick, he's not that fanged

revenant assailing nearby farm girls.
His bones are local. Afterlife is boundless,
the body held dear to the place of birth—

so the isotopes say, in Greek etymology
and mass spectrometry. Believe is the twin to
furlough, misplaced sharing the womb

with displaced. The teeth are chattering
to be replaced in the grounds he has, and be
reborn in cyclic systems breaking down.

# In the Wings

I chose to be awake. Due to bleed, and wrapped
in white, I feared my flow. My surgeons—men
with shot put arms, in sky blue scrubs—

who planned to cut and rearrange my jawbones
in the hours of a work day, knew this, but kept
me nude, per hospital rules, beneath sheets

as thick as X-ray blankets. In his house the night
before, the surgeon named like a pear fitted plaster
molds of my maxilla and mandible to a metal

frame that jiggled, lightly, like an unconscious me.
Small saws whirred, and he moved clean plaster
bones by millimeters to overlap without

my flow of blood from under gums. That morning
would be the repeat procedure, already rote.
I liked these details. I taught my men to tell me

the truth, to wreck imagination's dark spread.
The other surgeon had given up Olympic Track &
Field for medical school, to pull teeth

from gripping bone instead of putting metal balls
on grassy sectors. An orderly spun me through
corridors, up an elevator, to wait in a bright white,

kind of gurney chapel where I occupied
the interstitial spaces ahead of anesthesia.
The braces on my teeth would be laced

with wires to keep my mouth shut for six weeks
of healing. I was to be 24 in a month. Adulthood
was new. The last time I'd been there, at Overlook

Hospital, was to be born. Tucked in tight folds,
and lying flat, I felt the space was empty.
A pilot piped up across the room, talked knee

surgeries with a woman due for her first;
their voices loud like in bars—free in finding
common ground. No word from me.

Always a quiet one, I liked to be undercover.
I saw dust socializing in long rays from high
windows, and soon floated to the operating

theater to men with precision strength
wearing masks and telling jokes. My monthly
blood would wait past the next day to shed.

In ICU, one 3:00 am, sticky swallowed blood
caked the passages of tubing down my swollen
nose and throat. Nurses in bright cardigans

circled—*don't worry, they're just observing,*
said the Respiratory, in violet, as she watched
my screen heart jump, and touched my arm,

and vacuumed. I drifted back to the chapel bar
of rolling beds, when listening to flights
of conversation, all I wanted was to be aware.

## MATTER IN THE SCATTER

Why is the sky everywhere, asks the worried boy
trudging up Carroll past a 3-door black trash bin

taller than him, cartooned knapsack balanced between
thin backbones. Red brick corners cut with painted
black iron, splotchy London planes blooming electric

green against that nickel, milk, and delphinium-casted
cumulus and stratus. Why's the sky everywhere,

asks his elated dad, turning to greet this newly-voiced
category of concern before turning the idea inside out.

Because the sky is all around us. Walking past, I'm left
wondering if it is too early for one who can't tie shoelaces
to grasp the sun's broadcast through thick vapor into blue

and yellow particles? Or even astronomy, held fierce
as he is by gravity to a tipped slab on some planet

secretly spinning in space. I'm guessing the answer
is just embrace in place of outer space. We are matter —
and we do — held lightly in the Rayleigh Scatter.

## NUN OTHER

She predates blue robed Mary.
Her brush graces vellum with the brightest skies

above the apostles, paints marine haloed saints,
or *blue-tipped, long winged symbols hovering*

*over the evangelists.* Once again,
we had to unearth her expertise to believe it.

From the burnt rubble of a monastery in Dalheim,
a mandible's incisors inlaid with lazuli illuminate

a woman as exalted artist. Not a maid
grinding stone pigments for her master, a monk,

then wiping mouth and licking grit. These faded deposits
in fossilized tartar were mined beyond the sea.

It's the early 11th century. She ingests cochineal wings
and dried fish eyes, too, from crimson and glue.

She can paint stories that bloom in the text for all to see.
Or maybe she dates the blue of Mary, her brush turning

the once dark mourning robes ultramarine—
lazurite paste kneaded and blended with linseed

and lye, its aura trapped in small pots passed
in pockets and palms across Afghanistan,

tossed in vessel drawers on fraught seas
for trade in Venice, and coating the brush she kisses

to its finest point, particles settling in gum valleys.
She's quite a production, this middle-aged woman

in the high Middle Ages not given in marriage to a man;
she's evidence she mattered — even if she was sent

from the inlet of last daughters, her family
choosing for her a life of education and obedience.

More precious than gold that, in leaf, she floats
on puffs of humid breath down to the kingdom

of the text, a calculus of true blue reveals
her prominence above men's signatures of the age.

Was it humility that kept a nun's value occulted?
It could be the fire that swallowed her name

in a later raid. Maybe her artistry made her
recognizable while she lived, working in the light.

She sits back, satisfied, stretches her arms, sore
muscles, and sips ale, swishing that divine lapis lazuli.

## Tea Time

A Xi'an emperor who'd unburdened his subjects
of too much tax and upper classes, was —

to the ancient-worlders' delight—buried with his tea
buds, not just two chariots and the driving horses,

millet from his North, rice from his South, cross-
bows, spears, and knives, ceramic pigs, oxen,

elephants, unicorn, ducks, and unglazed, female
servants, bowed and peering. As now, too, in

141 BC, a fine floral brew revives the mind at prayers,
if not the breath, on the clop clop to enlightenment.

# Sipping Cappuccino at the Hair Salon

Junko's espresso hair falls to a hesitancy above her hip.
She can't bear to cut it, and says when it grays, she won't cover it.

I like the idea of the colorist who resists.

I sip froth from a demitasse spoon, wait for my cappuccino to cool
in its thick-walled, white porcelain cup. The stylists reflected
move in misremembered salsa steps around the heads they clip.

More low lights this time, I say, and point to one light swirl
in the rough-hewn planks around the mirrors. She frowns.

Junko blends bleach with colors, plasters a few hidden strands
of my gray and faded blond to a foil square she scores and folds.

I desire to sip the roasted spicy cappuccino before it gets cold,
and lean forward with half a head of flapping silver.
Wrigley's packets, sterling birds.

What happens to the used foil? Magpies poisoned by plucking glitter?

*Himitsu* means secret in Japanese, Junko tells me when I answer what
kind of poetry I write, with: I like hidden links and double meaning.

I'd also said walnuts for color. Not the shell, but nuanced like the nut.
Why didn't I point to the beverage that translates to capuchin?
Named not directly for the monkey with the high lights of intellect,

but the hood of the friar secreted away with his haywire belief.

Regardless, Junko gets it precisely. She makes me a *himitsu*.

## See Through

Lapis lazuli was in the chroma of the heavens,
reflected in the Nile, hard to come by, and carve.

Stone pigments degraded and faded from bright
shades. Pharaohs sought their own values
between green and violet, to endure as deities,

the ever-present blues. They put artisans to task
crushing malachite with sand and chalk to make

balls fired to frit, and ground to *hsbd iryt,*
that aspirational hue, Egyptian blue.
A transporting pigment, it powered all it dressed

with divinity. Amulets of the feisty hippopotamus
goddess of childbirth, horizon, and afterlife,

shimmered like sunlit sky in dynastic burial
chambers, each with one leg broken
to prevent harm to those it guided to the next world.

Belief is departure, being leaving all sense to trust.
No matter the fracture, a siege of faience stood unready

to guide the chosen to their brightest new existence.
Instead invention—*invenire, into, come*—lights
the way for New Kingdom artisans to slip through.

Is it possible everyone knew five millennia ago
that calcium copper tetra silicate reflects infrared

radiation—waves in lengths surpassing visible light?
If *artificial lapis lazuli* can surveil after dark, secure
currencies against forgery, and look inside you

at your little Niles of changing blood flow,
wouldn't it portray an avenue through the underworld?

No. But, at just one molecule, its value is outlasting
the prized metamorphic rock now out of time
on the market—currency to armed terrorists when mined

from Badakhshan—a conflict mineral to be denied
after 6,500 years of trade. The cool blue from the tomb heat

in the red land, radiates its hiding power, its revelation.

PERCEPTION

Sometimes a cloudy mirror,
the Gowanus looked like a stream
in a dell on that holiday I was not
observing, despite its oil tar,
and November's bite. I was not observing
well, lost beyond the scene. Dolly,
on leash, sat still in that fading day—
but she framed things differently.
I stood on the old Carroll Street
retractile bridge—bright as lazurite
and flanked by its chipped white gates
with red kisses. I turned to go,
and spotted a raccoon the size of my dog,
paused in its forward step.

Paused in its forward step
along the ridge outside the fence
by Alex Figliolia Plumbing —"We Subcontract
to Nobody"—a woodland animal stared
at my seated, self-assured terrier-collie
that neither growled nor barked.
The only noise was mine.
And like a portly dancer on the boards,
raccoon waltzed backwards without a slip;
his stare, or glare—or hers—
not retracted. Each had urges equal
to go for the throat I disrupted.
While I live in this constructed city,
sometimes it's a wilderness.

Sometimes it's a wilderness
out there: opossum curled in trash lid,
raccoons scaling fire escapes, egrets
hunting blue crab when camouflaged
in graffiti tags. I called Audubon, too,
about a hurt swan pedaling the oily canal.
Its mate and cygnet were gone, my neighbor said,

dashing off to dress the opera singers,
but urging me to ask. Ann was sure hungry hosts
were serving swans with sweet potatoes.
Swans fly, said the mellow man answering
bird calls in Prospect Park's chapter. Not captive,
nor prone. Sometimes, perception is all clear,
sometimes a cloudy mirror.

## Nursery of Divine Flowers

Almost imagined     the giant in white apron bowing
to present a pink carnation

on a vast green where long fragrant houses hard to breathe in
stood hidden in the open behind a row of two stories
with front walks and forsythias

Always sunny when we went there
my smiling mother Diantha and I shy beloved

Petunias impatiens geraniums roses
pansies begonias tiger lilies phlox irises baby's breath daisies
    I only remember carnations
not marigolds violets hibiscus day lilies delphinium ferns

I tried to find it when I could drive
the vanished nursery of corsages and boutonnière
its entry invisible     or not there     the street map mum

How small I was   it was   panoramic sugar egg
never where I thought it was

Almost remembered by anyone imagined     a field
like an estate that couldn't be there     windows
like glasses sloshed with milk
at the end of the long drive by a row of trees

Always sunny and only spring
when half school days met bouquets     red or   white   or pink
white shirts and starched aprons black shoes

Frisky buds on knotty green stems topped in bunched petals wrapped
in shiny dull paper by old giants who smiled at her   bowed
to present me one     I only remember carnations
My mother was one      I leaned against her knotty knees
dianthus  flower of Zeus       divine

# CROSSWINDS

I had been in a fold at winter's end,
February creased into March, the Sea

of Cortez and its emerging Blues, long
desert drive past mines, sea, and volcanoes—

with vapor that powered a region—to
a peninsula almost unpeopled, and in a lagoon

of mothering grey whales, while coronavirus,
and hubris, infected Italy and eased into

North America. Crosswinds always blew,
with little to suffer the argument—metal frames

held up tents scattered like little white
game piece houses on the scrub of a strange

board. We did not yet think the spreading
could suffocate and decrease us, as we put on pairs

of waterproof pants, sunscreen, and white galoshes,
to wade out to pool blue fishing boats that fit six,

secure in microbiologists and social contracts
honored. The grey whales swam near enough

for contact and stitched their flexible weights
under us, threading up to meet our spread hands.

Tucked in non tech on land, we only shared
with each other and our tour guides, perused

books: *Lagoon Time, Dolphin Mysteries,*
and *A Field Guide to the Stars and Planets.*

Out there, a breaching whale was the only server,
his body slap sending messages on alternate

currents in that biosphere reserve. Exhales and
breaking waves infused our senses, a sound symbiosis

I can still parse in my ear's mind. It is far too quiet
on the empty streets after New York City's lockdown:

an absence in which I am present, as elsewhere,
the mates, and the mothers with babes

in the San Ignacio Lagoon continue to migrate
from their brief season of affection.

## THE BLOWS

I'm tended to by winds,
wrapped in gauzes, hair brushed
and coiffed in sea salt sprays.

The sky is glowing, shrouded.
See the way it isn't light—not dawning
yet but reflected, near—in shades
of pencil sketch?

Between these soft, attentive
gusts I hear twin sprays of mist.
I'll hear them in a sighing city bus
stopped at next week's curb.

What is night for whales
refilling lungs each quarter hour?
I want to save this sense to buffer sirens
through meditated wafts and sprays.

But capture doesn't matter:
I return just days before lockdown
to weirder hush, week two of March,
shelves emptying except for fruit

and greens that no one wants.
Beer, canned foods, coffee.
Abundance perishing, as we will be,
in depleting present, taking the blows.

As we will be depleting, present,
taking blows of suffocating infection,
and socially stuck with our most
recent phases—as mine to be

alone except for one gray tabby,
sleeping her deepest without midnight
trucks, and laughing revelers.
Baja's whales and winds go on blowing.

# What There Is To See

—Waterfront Barge, Brooklyn, 2021

Rain combs nimbostratus across the meeting rivers.
I want to stay until the drops; cold April rustles
my own interior. Only as fog envelops this hushed
horizon do I see the indelible oil ships stalking

the harbor, visible as thick dashes—oil chips off
a palette knife, as if Winsor Newton, "Whale Strike."
Echoing, a T-Top zips across to the North River.
It may be the only one of its species in this month's

harbor. Liberty raises her hand for a ride she can't catch.
Her armor patination is a part of her corrosion. Made
from *living metal*, she's cyan by seacoast, alloys emergent
and healing. A yellow rope pulled taut along the narrow

stern is like a no-passing line on a paved street, and
port side, sky blue rope circles a yellow bitt as artisan
snood on a jug-eared man. It's high tide. Canadians
of an avian sort are pepped and vocal, sheltered

between this wooden waterfowl and the rocks. One
pedals leeward on his own slant, as if towards another
of his species behind the scrim of encroaching cloud
untucked and draped across the meeting rivers.

## Wild Borough

Waterfront blushes, it's time to leave. Low tide moves across the floor.
The city opens one puncture more. Earlier a skylight of day blue

and tissue moon, metronomic mast of tethered sailboat. Energy captivates
the space, shapes my feet today when last Friday, high tide, this flat bottom

boat was as solid as a foundation. Last day visiting Lehigh 79 Railroad
Barge docked in Red Hook in a fresh, shivery April. I need the light

for when I walk on Mill Street, a fenced sidewalk with a traffic light
and public service posters —What's good Brooklyn?—under the BQE,

past a gas station, the church where Al Capone got married, and the subway
garden with its individual plots above rumbling tunnels, but I linger

for persimmons and greys, tints of thistle, slippery blue, yolk, the doors
on every side open to the shifting water. The captain and his wife visit

with their daughter and her mate, talk about pizza toppings. The daughter
who used to ride bikes with her sister inside the barge, looping past

the microwave and the old ship gauges, salvaged propellers, the father who
gave them separate spaces on the roof with walkie-talkies as they grew

in and out of distances. I pack my journals, pen, and water-soluble pencils.
And what's that sound like metal scraping metal? Wing of the walkway

flexing in wind? Almost like the intake of breath on the little vaults
of a harmonica. But no, it is a goose I hear speaking out in the briefly

brightening, darkening harbor free of traffic, by the wild borough's bank.

## Day's Eyes

Riding under boroughs
express train

rising briefly beside me

a moment rose again
unbidden: little me cross-legged

and bored, not napping

slips into violet ocean with koi and galaxy
turns and waves through pages

Paul Klee picture book opened

while my mother sleeps
through migraine in the next room.

Here's a water tower

underneath a daisy
growing toward the riverbed.

I cross the platform to another line.

It was she who gave abstract art to her baby
an artist not living the art life

compelling me to.

# BREATHING SPACE

—2021

We turn out over the Atlantic, where one white sliver
and one bright skirt of speed flecks the ultramarine

elsewhere emptied of boats, near 9:00, hanging north
to start the long descent to Boston, widening east

to adjust for the stretched diagonal downward to meet
coordinates of far runway — shifts that feel as if I'm folded

tightly into an origami square balloon, then inflated to each
angle, ear and eye, now falling, floating in place —

when I see the miniature shape of large black whale
inhaling air in JetBlue's rhyming shadow this August

of traveling again, likely in a pod diving and rising east
of my spy, but out of sight on our next tilted turn.

FLIGHT

Why be afraid of flying
when sitting in the front of a canoe?
Illusion makes my rib cage
ache. I pause in this mirror pond.

When sitting in the front of a canoe,
I tumble out of sky's cumulus
ache. I pause in this mirror pond,
holding the paddle like a paintbrush.

I tumble out of sky's cumulus
mind and reflect on this scene
holding. The paddle-like paintbrush
disappears in lakes of cloud dispersing

mind, and I reflect on the scene
illusion makes. My rib cage
disappears. Lakes of cloud disperse.
Why be afraid of flying?

ABUNDANCE

I could only see the white-eyebrowed waves,
like quick chalk strikes on faces of charcoal
North Atlantic, and not the sprays — two fin

whales breathing ahead. I did see intricate dots
of snow float close and melt; one, three, no more.

From Nordic tongues, the word *sky* is *cloud*
and that surrounds this time sweep at ocean.
Under a younger gannet, its wing, torso —

I've seen plenty — is the mottled palette of this
cloud January, 100 miles from Belmar, before
the floor drops in canyon. Some folk will sleep

on these blue vinyl seats, in May, to wake further
out at dawn for puffin, petrel, skua, and Risso's.

If sinuses were blowing up ahead, then the fins
swam beneath us. Whale island, for a tick, our fin
transport. Someone saw a Minke in Jamaica Bay

the week before. Isn't it always yesterday, last week?
Beneath the fins I did not see, so often fins I might.

INTELLIGENCE

In shallow marsh beside the iron rails, an azure
crested, wing-tipped heron stands, unmoved by the blur of itself
writ large—azure crested Amtrak coursing low; alert instead
to small carp and green frogs. Did it catch in its complicated eye
that telescopes and microscopes in blinks right through
slippery surface glare, my open mouth in one passing square?
Eyes open day one, even if all it sees are apertures of plume.
Great blues hatch as compact chicks whose necks uncoil the evening
of their second day, extending views; actually, a folding vertebrae
equips a keen, quick hunter. Astute *Ardea herodias* knows where to be
to be unseen by what it wants—and not—in cattails, and bluing hues;
it's not shy about a steel predator speeding a fixed course.
At the optometrist, I, too, learned the brain chooses how it sees
(through multifocal contact lenses), the circles of remoteness and propinquity.

# NOTES

Page 16, "Bird Hearts Racing." Burd, ME, from OE, *bryd*, bride; chiefly Scottish, "a young woman."

Page 18, "Contributor." A few lines are sourced from "All Things Bright and Beautiful", by Cecil Francis Alexander. The tear photographer is Rose-Lynn Fisher. The sea turtle activist is Marc Ward.

Page 20, "How to Make a Whale Out of an Envelope." The aftermath of the Deep Water Horizon Oil Spill is referenced in this poem, which takes its title from a list of possible "How-To" article titles on a writers site.

Page 26, "My Mother Contributes to Force and Reaction." An ekphrastic poem from Rob Mulholland's 2013 sculpture, "Elemental Skytower", polished 316L stainless steel. The artist wrote about "the balance between order and chaos, force and reaction observed and reflected" in it.

Page 29, "Vestige." An ekphrastic poem from Rob Mulholland's 2009 polished 316L stainless steel sculpture "Vestige."

Page 30, "Reckless Endangerment." The photograph referenced at the start was taken by John Roca, and the police officer was Detective Martin Duffy. Caroline Domingo did actually report herself thinking "I'm not seeing this" when she spotted Ming for the first time. Judge Budd Goodman is also quoted in the poem. Mitochondrial Eve is a term in human genetics for the matrilineal most recent common ancestor of all living humans.

Page 35, "Let Them Be Endangered." "Koalas Aren't Extinct but their Futures are in Danger" (*New York Times*, November 25, 2019) and "Koala epidemic provides lesson in how DNA protects itself against viruses" (Science Daily, October 10, 2019).

Page 40, "Drawing out a Drawska Vampire." References a news story from October 2014 on the isotope analysis of skeletal remains treated to vampire burials, in Drawska, Poland, during a 19th c. cholera epidemic. Because certain individuals died within a day, they were thought to be vampires, and presumed to be strangers. Isotope analysis determines where someone originates.

Page 44, "Nun Other." References a news story from January 2019 of the discovery of powdered lapis lazuli stuck in the fossilized tartar of a jaw belonging to a woman who lived sometime between 900 and 1100, during the high Middle Ages.

Page 48, "See Through." The ancient Egyptian word *hsbd iryt* translates to "artificial lapis lazuli", the pigment we call Egyptian blue that was invented around 5,000 years ago. Details from the article "From Egyptian Blue to Infrared" in *Archaeology*, May/June 2013, are also referenced.

Page 58, "Day's Eyes." This poem refers to two Paul Klee artworks: "Fish Magic", oil and watercolor on panel, 1925; and "Night Flowers Submerged", lithograph, 1967. Daisy, OE, means "the day's eye."

ACKNOWLEDGMENTS

I am grateful to the journal and press editors who published many of these poems, some in earlier versions.

*The 5-2: Crime Poetry Weekly:* Rabbit Girl; Bird Hearts Racing; and How to Make a Whale Out of an Envelope

*BigCityLit*: Nature

*Blueline*: Flight

*The Chiron Review*: Sipping Cappuccino at the Hair Salon

*The Ekphrastic Review*: My Mother Contributes to Force and Reaction

*Gargoyle*: Goat Gardeners Take the High Ground at Brooklyn Bridge Park; Intelligence; and Wild Borough

*The Lake*: Matter in the Scatter; and Tea Time

*Live Nude Poems*: My Mother Made Herself the Deer with a Broken Leg

*Milk Newsletter (Poetry Society of New York):* A Small Invasion

*Mystic River Review:* Snowies and Blues

*The Night Heron Barks:* Nun Other

*Nixes Mate:* Breathing Space

*The SAME:* The Heart Is Quiet

*The Westchester Review:* Retreat; and Drawing out a Drawska Vampire

"Snowies and Blues" was also published in *Verse Daily*, March 28, 2005, in my prizewinning chapbook, *Wait for Me, I'm Gone* (Dream Horse Press, 2005), and the anthology, *And We the Creatures*, edited by C.J. Sage (Dream Horse Press, 2003).

"No One There" was in *Birds Fall Silent in a Mechanical Sea*, edited by Jane Ormerod, James Fucaloro, David Lawton, and George Wallace (great weather for MEDIA, 2019).

An earlier version of "Fret", entitled "Tracking Humpbacks in Barra de Potosí" was in the anthology, *Like Light: 25 Years of Bright Hill Press Poetry & Prose*, edited by Bertha Rogers (Bright Hill Press, 2017).

"Rabbit Girl" was reposted in the *Gowanus Patch Newsletter* inside an interview with me by the reporter, Marc Torrence, who had written the original article that inspired the poem.

I am grateful to Gerald So, editor of *The 5-2: Crime Poetry Weekly*, for nominating "How to Make a Whale Out of an Envelope" for Best of the Net, and to Lesleigh Forsyth, former poetry editor at *The Westchester Review*, for nominating "Drawing Out a Drawska Vampire" for a Pushcart Prize.

"What There Is To See" and "Wild Borough" were written from my April 2021 Poets Afloat micro-residency on the Lehigh 79 railroad barge docked in Red Hook, Brooklyn. Much appreciation to Brad Vogel for creating this program on historic boats in the New York Harbor, and to David Sharps, director of The Waterfront Barge Museum, for the time, space, and conversation on two April Fridays in the spring of gradual reopening after New York's pandemic shutdown.

It's vital to have the eyes and minds of other poets reading/reeling in one's poems, and I appreciate the members of the Urban Rangers writing group who urged me to find the core and diction of several poems: Ruth Danon, Sally Dawidoff, Elisabeth Frost, David Groff, Melissa Hotchkiss, Stephen Massimilla, Hermine Meinhard, Suzanne Parker, Soraya Shalforoosh, and Elaine Sexton. When writing the manuscript seemed plodding and mysterious, I was fortunate to have the voices of confident friends believing that, of course, there was a book, especially Jennifer Hecht, Lisa Andrews, Hilary Sideris and Saundra Norton.

Much appreciation and gratitude to Ruth Thompson and Don Mitchell for the wonderful experience of publishing a book with Saddle Road Press.

## About the Author

Amy Holman is a poet, prose writer, literary consultant, and artist. *Captive* is her sixth poetry book. She is the author of the collection, *Wrens Fly Through This Opened Window*, and four chapbooks, including the prizewinning *Wait for Me, I'm Gone*.

She was a 2021 NYC Poets Afloat micro-residency fellow on a historic boat in the New York harbor. Her poems have been on *Verse Daily* and in *The Best American Poetry*, and nominated by journal editors for Best of the Net and Pushcart Prizes. She grew up in northern New Jersey, and lives in Brooklyn, New York.

She also writes the substack newsletter, What Where: Literary Journals for poets and fiction writers.

amy-holman.com